SCRIPTURAL CATECHISM

Fr. Herbert Burke

A HELPFUL RESOURCE FOR
R.C.I.A. AND C.C.D. or FAITH FORMATION PROGRAMS

FULLY INDEXED TO THE
"CATECHISM OF THE CATHOLIC CHURCH"

A SCRIPTURAL CATECHISM

Fr. Herbert Burke

A HELPFUL RESOURCE FOR
R.C.I.A. AND C.C.D. or FAITH FORMATION PROGRAMS

FULLY INDEXED TO THE
"CATECHISM OF THE CATHOLIC CHURCH"

Queenship

PUBLISHING COMPANY
P.O. Box 220 • Goleta, CA 93116
(800) 647-9882 • (805) 692-0043 • Fax: (805) 967-5133

Nihil Obstat:
Rev.Isidore Dixon, S.T.D.
Censor Deputatus

Imprimatur:
Most Rev.William E.Lori, S.T.D.
Vicar General for the Archdiocese of Washington

May 3, 1995

The nihil obstat and imprimatur are official declarations that a book or pamphlet is free of doctrinal or moral error. No implication is contained therein that those who have granted the nihil obstat and the imprimatur agree with the content, opinions or statements expressed.

Library of Congress Number # 2004113657

Published by:
Queenship Publishing
P.O. Box 220
Goleta, CA 93116
(800) 647-9882 • (805) 692-0043 • Fax: (805) 967-5133
www.queenship.org

Printed in the United States of America

ISBN: 1-57918-268-2

Written in Honor of Mary,
Queen of the Most Holy Rosary

Table of Contents

Part I The Creed

Part II The Seven Sacraments

Part III The Commandments

Part IV Prayer

Appendix

Part I

The Creed

Jesus said to her, 'I am the resurrection and the life; he who believes in me, though he die, yet shall he live, and whoever lives and believes in me shall never die.' (John 11:25, 26)

What is the Purpose of Life?

[Cross Reference:1-3, 1718, Catechism of the Catholic Church]

We were created to be perfectly happy forever with God. Perfect happiness can only be found in perfect life, love, and truth, which is God. Happiness does not exist in temporary and imperfect, material possessions (Lk.12:15), sensual pleasures (Ec.1:8), and human friendships, but only in perfect and eternal friendship with God. *Do not lay up for yourselves treasures on earth, where moth and rust consume and where thieves break in and steal, but lay up for yourselves treasures in heaven, where neither moth nor rust consumes and where thieves do not break in and steal. For where your treasure is, there will your heart be also. Therefore do not be anxious, saying, 'What shall we eat?' or 'What shall we drink?' or 'What shall we wear?' For the Gentiles [Unbelievers] seek all these things; and your heavenly Father knows that you need them all.* **But seek first his kingdom and his righteousness,** *and all these things shall be yours as well.* (Matt. 6:19-21, 31-33)

St.Augustine : "You have made us for yourself, O Lord, and our hearts are restless until they rest in you."

How do I Know God Exists?
[31-38]

From the greatness and the beauty of created things their original author, by comparison, is seen. (Wis.13:1-9) (Rom.1:18-22)

How Can We experience God?
[2558-2565]

By opening our hearts in prayer and asking for His Holy Spirit to come into our heart and life, and by turning our backs on sin (Lk.11:13). *Draw near to God, and he will draw near to you.* (Jas.4:8) *Behold, I stand at the door and knock. If any man listens to my voice and opens the door to me, I will come in to him and will sup with him, and he with me.* (Rev.3:20)

What is the Gospel?
[124-129, 571]

For God so loved the world that he gave his only Son, that whoever believes in him should not perish but have eternal life. (Jn.3:16) ...the power of God for salvation to every one who has faith. (Rm.1:16)

Why does God allow evil?
[309-324]

1. (To test us) (Job.1, 2, 38-42, 1Pt.4:12-18).

2. (To preserve free will) (Sir.15:14-17, Gal.6:7, 8)

3. (To draw good out of evil) (Gen.50:20, Ezek.33:11)

4. (Through the great evil of the crucifixion He brought about the great good of redemption) (Lk.24:26, Is.53:11, 12)

5. (To conquer evil) (Rom.12:21)

6. (To give us a means to a greater reward) "He who overcomes, I will permit him to sit with me upon my throne; as I also have overcome and have sat with my Father on his throne." (Rev.3:21, Job.42:10,12.)

7. (Why do we allow evil?)

Divine Revelation
[50-141]

Divine Revelation is the Word of God. It is the truth God reveals to us about Himself and what we need to know to enter heaven. Divine Revelation comes to us through Sacred Tradition **and** Sacred Scripture (2 Thess. 2:15).

Sacred Tradition
[75-79]

Tradition is the spoken Word of God passed on from Christ to the Apostles and from the Apostles to the Church (2 Thess.2:15, 1Cor.11:2, Matt.28:19). It is found in the Creed, Church Council Documents, and writings of Popes, Church Fathers and Doctors. (See also:1 Cor.11:2, Gal.1:8-9, 2Thess.2:15, 3:6, 2Tim.l:13, 2:2, 3:14.)

Sacred Scripture
[101-141]

Sacred Scripture is the written Word of God; it contains the history of salvation. *All scripture is inspired by God, and useful for teaching.* (2.Tim.3:16) God is the primary Author of Sacred Scripture (The Bible).

If you have never read the Bible before, I recommend that you start with Luke, John, and Acts.

The Apostle's Creed:
A Short Summary of God's Revelation
[185-197]

I believe in God the Father Almighty, Creator of heaven and earth; and in Jesus Christ, His only Son, Our Lord; Who was conceived by the Holy Spirit, born of the Virgin Mary, suffered under Pontius Pilate, was crucified, died, and was buried. He descended into hell; on the third day He arose again from the dead. He ascended into heaven, and is seated

4

at the right hand of the Father. He will come again to judge the living and the dead. I believe in the Holy Spirit, the Holy Catholic Church, the communion of saints, the forgiveness of sins, the resurrection of the body, and life everlasting. Amen.

Bible Only Theory
[82]

The Catholic Church rejects the "Bible only" theory because the Bible cannot interpret itself (Acts 8:27-31, 2Pt.1:20, 21, 3:16). The fact that many Bible Christians disagree on such important issues as abortion, divorce, and infant baptism, is enough to prove that the Bible cannot stand alone and explain itself; there must be a central authority to interpret it. We believe the Church is authorized by God since scripture calls the Church, *the pillar and mainstay of the truth* (1Tim.3:15). God guided the Church to decide which books would make up the Bible at the Council of Carthage in 396 A.D. God guides this same Church to interpret it. One Christian with a copy of the Bible cannot interpret doctrine for himself which contradicts the Church any more than a citizen with a copy of the Constitution has authority to interpret it for the U.S. without the guidance of the Supreme Court. The "Bible only" theory is not taught by the Bible, was never taught by the apostles, and didn't exist until 1500 A.D.

Science and Religion
[2293, 2294]

Science is limited to the physical world and cannot explain or reveal spiritual realities. Science can tell us how things are made, but not who made them or why. Science cannot tell us what is right or wrong, or what we should live for, only Divine Revelation can.

Who is God?
[198-231]

God is our Father (Is.64:7)

God is our Creator (Gen.1:1)

God is our Savior (Lk.1:47)

God is Eternal (Ps.90:2, 4)

God is all Powerful [*Omnipotent*] (Lk.1:37)

God is all Knowing [*Omniscient*] (1Sam.2:3)

God is Present Everywhere *[Omnipresent]* (Ps.139:7-12)

God is all Good [*Omnibenevolent*] (Ps.136:1)

God is Just (Ps.119:37)

God is Holy (Lev.19:2)

God is One (Mk.12:29, 32)

God is the Father, Son, and Holy Spirit (Mt.28:19)

The Holy Trinity
[232-267]

The Holy Trinity is a mystery; we can only have a partial understanding of it. God possesses one nature made up of three Divine Persons. A nature is what something or someone is. A person is who someone is. God is one Divine Nature, but He is Three Divine Persons: God the Father, God the Son, and God the Holy Spirit (Mt.28:19, Gen.3:22)

Jesus Christ
[422-682]

Jesus Christ is the Eternal Son of God, the Second Divine Person of the Holy Trinity, Who became man for our salvation. His death paid our debt for sin, and merited Eternal life for us. Dying, He destroyed our death; rising ,He restored our Life. Jesus is both God and Man, both "Son of God" and "Son of Man". Scripture teaches that Christ is Divine: (Col.2:9, Jn.1:1, 5:18, 10:30, 20:28, Is.9:5, 6, Matt.1:23)

He is "the Son of God" (Mt.4:3), "the Savior of the world" (Jn.4:42) and, "The lamb of God who takes away the sin of the world." (Jn.1:29) Of Himself He says:

I am the Alpha and the Omega, the beginning and the end. (Rv.21:6)

I am the resurrection and the Life; he who believes in me, even if he die, shall live. (Jn.11:25)

I am the Way, and the Truth, and the Life. No one comes to the Father but through me. (Jn.14:6)

I am the bread of Life. (Jn.6:35)

I am the light of the world. (Jn.8:12)

I am the door. (Jn.10:7)

I am the good shepherd. (Jn.10:11)

I am the true vine. (Jn.15:1)

Before Abraham came to be- I AM. (Jn.8:58, cf.Ex.3:14)

God the Holy Spirit
[683-747]

The Holy Spirit is the Divine Third Person of the Holy Trinity. The scriptures say:

The Holy Spirit is God (John 4:24, Acts 5:3, 4, John 4:24, Gen 6:3).

The Holy Spirit is the Spirit of truth (John 14:17).

The Holy Spirit is the Spirit of God (Matt.3:16, Gen.1:2).

The Holy Spirit is the Spirit of life (Romans 8:2\Rev.11:11).

The Holy Spirit dwells within the servants of God (Ezek.36:27\1Cor.6:17\1Cor.3:16).

The Holy Spirit makes our bodies His Temple (1Cor.6:19, 20).

The Holy Spirit is the Spirit of Love (2Tim.1:7\1John4:16).

The Spirit of Grace (Zech.12:10).

The Spirit of Holiness (2Thess.2:13).

The Spirit of Joy (1Thess.1:6\Rom.14:17).

The Holy Spirit is power from on High (Is.32:15\Luke24:49).

The Holy Spirit helps us under persecution (Matt.10:17-20\ Mark13:11\Luke 21:14, 15).

The Holy Spirit is given to those who believe in Jesus and keep his commandments. (1John3:23,24\1John4:13\ 1Cor.12:3\Acts5:29-32).

The Seven Gifts and Twelve Fruits of the Holy spirit
[1831,1832]

Seven Gifts

1. Wisdom
2. Understanding
3. Counsel
4. Fortitude
5. Knowledge
6. Piety
7. Fear of the Lord
(Is.11:2,3).

Twelve Fruits:

1. Charity
2. Joy
3. Peace
4. Patience
5. Kindness
6. Goodness
7. Long-suffering
8. Humility
9. Fidelity
10. Modesty
11. Continence
12. Chastity
(Gal. 5:22, 23, 24).

Angels: Messengers of God
[328-354]

Angels are Ministering spirits (Heb.1:14), created by God. Angels can appear to man as having a body (Tobit 12:19), and are described as having wings (Ex.25:20,37:9, Ezek.10:5). Everyone has a guardian angel to help protect him from spiritual and physical harm (Acts 12:15, Matt 18:10).

The Devil
[391-395]

The devil (Matt.4:1) was created as a good angel, but he chose to sin against God (Ezek.28:12-17, Is.14:11-15). He led a rebellion against God and some other angels followed him in this. They are called demons. (Rev.12:7-9)

Creation and The Fall of Man
[279-421]

In the beginning God created the heavens and the earth. (Gen.1:1). Man is a creature composed of body and soul, and created in the image of God. (Gen.1:26\2:7) The fall of man is his fall from grace into sin. Adam and Eve were the first man and woman created by God. They were created in grace or friendship with God. They were tempted by the devil to disobey God (Gen.3) and committed the first (original) sin. They lost their friendship with God, and were driven out of the Garden of Eden into a world of suffering and death—for them and their descendants. (Ps.51:7, Rom.5:12)

Grace
[1996-2005]

Grace is a necessary supernatural gift of God which confers new life onto the soul—God's own Divine life. We grow in grace through receiving the sacraments, through prayer, reading scripture, and performing acts of charity. We lose grace through sin. The two main types of grace are sanctifying grace and actual grace.

Sanctifying Grace
[2000]

Without sanctifying grace we cannot enter into heaven. It makes us holy and pleasing to God. Being filled with sanctifying grace makes us children of God and gives us a right to heaven. We should have sanctifying grace at all times.

Actual Grace
[2000]

Actual graces are special working graces sent to us as we need them to do good works or resist temptation.

Original Sin
[396-409]

Original sin is the sin of our first parents, which deprived us of grace and friendship with God. It has caused us to have a weakened will so that it is harder for us to do good and avoid evil. (Gen.3, Ps.51:7) Original sin is called "sin" in an analogical sense, since it is a sin that we have "contracted", but not "committed". It is a condition, not an action. It is not a "personal sin" or "actual sin" which we committed.

Actual Sin
[1849-1851]

Sin is an action against God's will and commandments. *He who knows how to do the right thing and does not do it commits sin.* (Jas.4:17) (1Jn.3:4). There are different degrees of sin: (Mt.5:19, Jn.19:11)

Mortal Sin
[1854-1874]

Mortal sin deprives the soul of sanctifying grace. Those who die with an unrepented mortal sin on their souls cannot enter heaven (1Jn.5:16, 17, Jn.15:6, Gal.5:19-21). There are three conditions necessary for a mortal sin:

1. **Serious matter**—the thought, word, action or omission must be seriously wrong or believed to be. (Lk.12:47, 48, Gen.20:1-8)

2. **Sufficient reflection**—the person must be mindful of the serious wrong (think about it before you do it).

3. **Full consent** (freely choose to commit the sin).

Venial Sin
[1862,1863]

Venial sin is a sin which does not involve serious matter,

or one in which one of the three conditions for a mortal sin is missing.

Occasion of Sin
[226]

A person, place, or thing which leads us to sin is an occasion of sin. (Mt.5:29, 30, Pr.4:14, 15, Sir.9:3-13)

The Church: The Body of Christ
[787-796]

The Church is: The Communion of Saints—Apostles' Creed (Heb.10:25), The Body of Christ (Eph.1:23, 1Cor.12:27), and the Family of God (Eph.3:15).

The Four Marks of the Church
[813-873]

One—All members believe one faith under the Pope (Eph.4:4-6, Jn.17:21).

Holy—Because of its teachings, its sacraments, and its founder, Christ.

Catholic—Universal, the same in doctrine for all people (Mt.28:19, 20).

Apostolic—it was founded through the Apostles (Eph.2:20, Rev.21:14).

The Pope
[552-567]

The word Pope means "Father". The Pope is the Chief Shepherd of the Church, he is the primary teacher and ruler. The Pope is the infallible interpreter of revelation for Catholics. The Pope is only infallible as Chief shepherd of the church when he clearly defines a matter concerning faith or morals. He does not make new revelation, but clarifies the original revelation of Christ and the Apostles. The Pope is not impeccable (incapable of sinning). Belief in infallibility is inescapable; it is not an option. We either believe the Pope, ourselves, or someone else to be the infallible (reliable) guide to scripture. We must trust in someone's interpretation of scripture. Catholics trust the Pope because He was appointed by Christ. *You are Peter, and upon this rock I will build my church, and the gates of hell will not prevail against it.* (Mt.16:17-19) *I have prayed for you that your faith may not fail.* (Lk.22:31, 32) Christ named him Peter "Cephas", which in Hebrew means "foundation stone". "I will give you the keys to the kingdom of heaven; and whatever you shall bind on earth shall be bound in heaven." (Mt.16:19) The "keys" symbolize authority (Is.22:15-25, Rv.1:18). He says to Peter: *Feed my sheep* (Jn.21:15-17) which means "teach my church." He appoints Peter as chief shepherd of His church. Christ is the invisible head of the Church, the Pope is the visible head. Scripture shows the first dispute over doctrine was settled by a church council (Acts 15) presided over by the first Pope (Acts15:7). This is the scriptural model for settling disputes over doctrine. Peter is listed first in every list of Apostles (Mt.10:1-4, Mk.3:16-19, Lk.6:12-16, Acts1:13), first to work a miracle in His name (Acts3:6-7), and first to preach the gospel (Acts2:14).

The Blessed Virgin Mary: The New Eve
[494]

Mary is called *Blessed* (Lk.1:42, 48) *Virgin* (Mt.1:23), *the Mother of Jesus* (Acts1:14), and the Mother of God. The Bible calls Christ the New Adam. *For as in Adam all die, so in Christ all will be made to live* (1Cor.15:22). The early Church Fathers called Mary the New Eve (Gen.3:15). As through Eves death came, so through Mary life came. A fallen angel deceived Eve, a sinless virgin (Gen.3:4); she disobeyed God and brought death to the world. A good angel gave truth to a sinless *virgin named Mary* (Lk.1:27); she obeyed God and brought life to the world. God uses the same instruments the devil used for our fall as the instruments for our redemption: two sinless sons of God—Adam (Lk.3:38) and Christ, two sinless virgins—Mary and Eve, two trees— the tree of knowledge and the cross, two angels—Devil and Gabriel.

Mary, the Mother of God
[495]

Mary is the Mother of God because she gave birth to Jesus who is both God and man. (Lk.1:43, Jn.20:28) Mary is our spiritual mother. (Jn.19:25-27, Rev.12:1, 17, Gen.3:20)

Immaculate Conception
[491-492]

The Immaculate Conception means that Mary was conceived without sin. This was to prepare her for a special role as the Mother of God, when she would conceive by the Holy Spirit (Luke 1:26-38\Matt 1:18, 19, 20). God chose to apply the anticipated merits of Jesus Christ to her soul at the moment of her conception and preserve her from original sin. In the beginning God created a sinless man and woman who fell; in the new beginning of redemption God would have another sinless man and woman who would never fall.

Mary's Perpetual Virginity
[496-510]

Mary is called a Perpetual Virgin because she was a virgin, before, during, and after the birth of Christ. (Luke 1:34, Isaiah 7:14) Note that the Greek term used for the "brothers" (Mk.3:31) of Jesus means cousin or brother.

Mary's Assumption into Heaven
[966,974]

Mary was assumed, body and soul, into heaven. Mary deserved the honor of being assumed into heaven because she was free of sin and its consequences. Elijah and Enoch were assumed into heaven (Gen.5:24, 2Kings 2, Heb.ll:5,6), and Mary had an even higher role in the plan of salvation.

The Intercession of Mary
[969-975]

Catholics worship only God, but they honor Mary as their spiritual Mother (Rev.12:1-17, Jn.19:26, 27). Mary is a creature, not the creator. However, Mary is the Mother of God (Lk.1:43, Jn.20:28). She is our Mother, and the Queen of Heaven. Lk.1:48: *For Behold, henceforth all generations will*

The Annunciation

In the sixth month the angel Gabriel was sent from God to a city of Galilee named Nazareth, to a virgin betrothed to a man whose name was Joseph, of the house of David; and the virgin's name was Mary. And he came to her and said, "Hail, full of grace, the Lord is with you!" Luke 1:26-28

The Birth of Christ

And she gave birth to her first-born son and wrapped him in swaddling cloths, and laid him in a manger, because there was no place for them in the inn. Luke 2:7

call me blessed. We are commanded by God to *Honor your Father and Mother* (Ex.20:12), thus the honor we give to Mary our Spiritual Mother in no way subtracts from the worship we give to God any more than honoring our earthly mother does. In fact, it conforms to God's holy will, and we who are sons of God honor her whom the Son of God honored.

Christ is our only mediator (1Tim.2:5-6) with the Father, but Mary can intercede (pray for us) with her Son Jesus. Jesus worked His first miracle at her request (Jn.2:1-12). Just as we can ask others members of the church on earth to pray for us (1Tim.2:1, 2Tim.1:3, Phil4, 22), so, too, can we ask members of the church in heaven to pray for us. (Rev.5:8, 6:9-11, 7:10-12, 8:2-6, Mat.22:31, 32). As a builder is honored when someone admires his work; God honored when we honor Mary. God loves us to honor Mary as a Father is pleased when his daughter is honored. All the honor we give to Mary is reflected back to God since we honor her for what He has done for her, with her, and through her. When we honor her we honor Him.

The Last Judgment
[1038-1041]

At death, each soul receives his own individual judgment by God. At the end of the world, Christ will return to the earth and judge it (Mt.25, Wis.1-5). He will restate the individual judgments we received at death in front of the whole world. At this time all the dead will rise (1Cor.15). *And I saw a great white throne and the one who sat upon it; from his face the earth and heaven fled away, and there was found no place for them. And I saw the dead, the great and the small,*

Jesus works His first Miracle through Mary's Intercession

When the wine failed, the mother of Jesus said to him, "They have no wine."... This, the first of his signs, Jesus did at Cana in Galilee, and manifested his glory; and his disciples believed in him. John 2:3, 11

standing before the throne, and scrolls were opened. And another scroll was opened, which is the book of life; and the dead were judged out of those things that were written in the scrolls, according to their works... And if anyone was not found written in the book of life, he was cast into the pool of fire. (Rv.20:11-13)

Heaven
[1023-1029]

Heaven is a place of reward and eternal happiness for those who do God's will on earth and die in a state of grace.

*Well done, good and faithful servant; because you have been
faithful over a few things, I will set you over many; enter into
the joy of your master.* (Mt.25:21) *And he said to Jesus, 'Lord,
remember me when you come into your kingdom.'And Jesus
said to him, 'This day you shall be with me in paradise.'*
(Lk.23:42, 43) (Rev.21:3, 4, 1Cor.2:9) There are different
degrees of reward in heaven because each receives according
to his works (Mk.4:20, 10:35-40, Lk.19:17, 19, 1Cor.3:8,
15:41, 42, 2Cor.9:6-8, Mt.16:27).

Hell
[1033-1037]

Hell is a place of eternal punishment for those who die in
a state of mortal sin and consequently have rejected God's
life, truth, and love. The two main punishments of hell are the
"pain of loss" (eternal loss of friendship with God) and the
"pain of sense"(eternal torment of the senses). *Depart from
me, accursed ones, into the everlasting fire prepared for the
devil and his angels.* (Mt.25:41) (Mk.9:42-47, Lk.16:19-31,
Mt.10:28)

Purgatory
[1030-1032]

Purgatory is a temporary place where souls go to complete penance which they did not complete on earth. *It is
therefore a holy and wholesome thought to pray for the dead,
that they may be loosed from their sins.* (2Mac.12:46)
(1Cor.3:11-15, Mt.5:23-26)

Part II
The Seven Sacraments
[1210-1666]

Do this in memory of me. (1Cor.11:24)

A sacrament is an outward sign instituted by Christ to give us grace. The sacraments are entrusted to the Church and given as a means by which divine life is dispensed to us. They give graces and bear fruit when we receive them with the proper disposition. Each sacrament has both form and matter. Form constitutes the words used in the administration of the sacrament; matter involves the pouring of water for baptism, bread and wine for mass, anointing with oil for confirmation and the anointing of the sick, contrition for confession, laying on of hands for ordination, and mutual consent for a couple choosing marriage.

1. **Baptism:** [1213-1284] The sacrament of Baptism (Mt.28:19, Jn.3:5) is the first sacrament we receive. It is necessary to receive before receiving the other sacraments.

Baptism forgives original sin, actual sin, and infuses sanctifying grace within the soul (Ezek.36:25, 26, Acts 2:38, 22:16, 1Cor.6:11, Gal.3:26, 27). It applies the merits of Christ's death on the cross to our souls, and cleanses us from sin. It makes us children of God, brothers of Christ, and temples of the Holy Spirit. It can be received only once and leaves an eternal mark upon the face of the soul.

2. **Confirmation:** [1285-1321] (Acts:8:14-17, 9:17-19, 19:5, 6, Ti.3:4-8) Along with Baptism and the Holy Eucharist, Confirmation is part of the triad of Christian initiation. Confirmation increases and deepens the graces received at baptism. It unites us more firmly to Christ and it increases the gifts of the Holy Spirit within us. It imparts a special strength to witness, spread, and defend the faith. It can be received only once and leaves an eternal mark upon the face of the soul.

3. **Holy Eucharist:** [1322-1419] (Jn.6:25-71, Mt.26:26-28, 1Cor.11:23-26, Lk.24:30, 31) The Holy Eucharist is also called "communion" and the "Blessed Sacrament". The Holy Eucharist is "the source and summit of the Christian life." (LG11) It is not a symbol, but is the Real Body, Blood, Soul, and Divinity of Jesus Christ. During the miracle of the Mass, the priest consecrates (changes) the bread and wine into the Body and Blood of Christ at the words of institution, taken from scripture, which are: *This is my Body; this is my Blood.* (1Cor.11:24, 25). The mass is a sacrifice because it re-presents or makes present in an unbloody manner the sacrifice of Christ on the cross at Calvary (Mal.1:10, 11, Heb.13:10). Christ said: *I am the living bread that has come down from heaven. If anyone eat of this bread he shall live forever; and*

*the bread that I will give is my flesh for the life of the
world...he who eats my flesh and drinks my blood has eternal
life and I will raise him up at the last day. For my flesh is
food indeed, and my blood is drink indeed. He who eats my
flesh and drinks my blood abides in me, and I in him.*
(Jn.6:48-56) The Holy Eucharist is a Paschal Banquet, a
sacrificial memorial of Christ's Passover (1Cor.5:7). If we
have committed a mortal sin, we must go to confession first,
before receiving communion. Otherwise, instead of bringing
grace to the soul, communion brings the sin of sacrilege
(1Cor.11:27-29). To receive communion, one must come
forward with his or her hands folded in prayer. When you
come before the priest, he will say:" The Body of Christ":
showing your belief, you respond," Amen". Then open your
mouth and receive on the tongue (ordinary way), or you place
out your hand, palm open resting on the other hand, to receive
on your hand, and immediately place the host in your mouth
(optional way).

4. **Penance:** [1422-1498] This sacrament is also called
Confession, or Reconciliation. (Prv.28:13, Matt.9:6-8) Christ
gave the power to forgive sins in His name to the Apostles,
and they passed this power on to their successors, the Bishops
and Priests. Confession forgives sins committed after baptism. When going to confession, one must confess all known
mortal sins according to kind (type, such as adultery or theft)
and number (amount, such as once, few, many). After confessing your sins, you listen to any advice the priest may
offer, pray the act of contrition, receive absolution (Christ's
forgiveness) from the priest, leave the confessional, and then
complete your penance (prayers or some other act of penance)
(2Sam.12:13, 14, 1Chr.21:8-13, Jas.5:20). The priest is bound

The Last Supper: The First Mass
"I am the living bread which came down from heaven; if any one eats of this bread, he will live for ever; and the bread which I shall give for the life of the world is my flesh." (John 6:51)

under pain of mortal sin not to reveal anything he has heard in confession. This is called the seal of the confessional. A priest would go to jail or die before he would reveal sins that someone confessed to him. (Luke 15, Ezk.33).

5. **Anointing of the Sick:** [1499-1532] This sacrament forgives sins and may promote physical healing, if it is God's will. (Mk.6:13, Jas.5:13-15).

6. **Holy Orders:** [1536-1600] (Gen.14:18, Heb.5:5-10, Lk.22:19, Acts.6:6, 14:22, 23) This Sacrament enables Christ's apostles and their successors to administer the Sacraments and serve the Church. There are three degrees of Holy Orders: 1.Deacon, 2.Priest, 3.Bishop. Only bishops can ordain, and only bishops and priests can administer the sacraments of confirmation, confession, anointing of the sick, and offer the Sacrifice of the Mass.

Why call priests Father? They are spiritual Fathers in the Church. They give life to people through proclaiming the Gospel and through the Sacraments. (1Cor.4:14-15, 1Thes.2:9-12)

Why are priests celibate? They follow the example and teaching of Jesus Christ (celibate priest), to sacrifice marriage for the kingdom. (Mt.19:12, Lk.18:29, 1Cor.7)

7. **Matrimony:** (Mk.10:2-12, Eph.5) This Sacrament joins a man and woman together for life by the power of God for the purpose of union (love) and procreation (life). Marriage is binding until death (1Cor.7:10, 11, 39, Mt.19:4-9). An Annulment is a declaration made by the church which states after a thorough investigation has been completed, that the elements necessary for a valid marriage were not present at the time of the wedding, and therefore no true marriage ever took place. It is not a divorce.

The Crucifixion

And when they came to the place which is called The Skull, there they crucified him, and the criminals, one on the right and one on the left. And Jesus said, "Father, forgive them; for they know not what they do." (Luke 23:33-34)

Part III

The Commandments

If you love me, you will keep my commandments. (John 14:15)

The Two Great Commandments:
[2055, 2083]

I. *You shall love the Lord your God with your whole heart, with your whole soul, and with all your mind. This is the first and greatest commandment. The second is like it.* (Deut.6:5, Mt.22:37-39) The first great commandment corresponds to the first 3 of the ten commandments given to Moses.

II. *You shall love your neighbor as yourself.* (Lev.18:9, Mt.22:37-39) The second great commandment corresponds to the last seven commandments.

The Ten Commandments:
(Ex.20:1-17, Deut.5:6-21)
[2084-2557]

1. *YOU SHALL HAVE NO FALSE GODS.* [2084-2141]
   This means we worship only the true God, especially
   through prayer, and do not give greater love to anything
   else.

2. *YOU SHALL NOT TAKE GOD'S NAME IN VAIN.*
   [2142-2167] Use only with reverence.

3. *KEEP THE SABBATH HOLY.* [2168-2195] Attend mass
   on Sundays and Holy Days of obligation, and abstain
   from unnecessary physical labor on Sunday.

4. *HONOR YOUR FATHER AND MOTHER.* [2196-2257]
   Love, help, respect, and obey your parents.

5. *YOU SHALL NOT KILL.* [2258-2330] We must take
   care of our bodies, and not unjustly injure others physi-
   cally or verbally.(Mt.5:21-26). Alcohol and drug abuse is
   sinful (Gal.5:21). We are allowed to defend ourselves;
   however, killing out of vengeance is wrong. Abortion is
   murdering innocent life (Lk.1:15, 41, 44, Ps.139:13,
   Is.13:18).

6. *YOU SHALL NOT COMMIT ADULTERY.* [2331-2400]
   *Blessed are the pure in heart, for they shall see God. You
   have heard that it was said, 'You shall not commit adultery.' But I say to you that every one who looks at a
   woman lustfully has already committed adultery with her
   in his heart.* (Mt.5:8, 27, 28) This commandment calls for

the virtue of chastity or purity and forbids all sexual sins: adultery, fornication (pre-marital sex) (Gal.5:16-24, 1Cor.6:15-20, Eph.5:5, 6, Mt.15:19, Rev.22:15), impure thoughts, pornography (Ps.101:3, Matt.5:27, Ezek.16:25), immodest dress (Is.3:16-24,1 Tim.2:9, 10, 1Pt.3:1-6), masturbation, homosexual acts (Gen.19:1-29, Mt.5:30, Rom.1:24-27, 1Cor.6:10, 1Tim.1:10), and contraception (Gen.38:8-10). Unlike Natural Family Planning, artificial birth control violates the natural design intended by God for sexuality, for God created conjugal relations to be life-giving. Contraception unnaturally separates the two goods of marriage, life (procreation) and love (union): (Gen.1:28, Ps.127:3-5,Gen.38:8-10, Ru.4:13) For information contact your local parish or diocesan family planning office.

The sin of fornication (pre-marital sex) is the use of the marital act outside of marriage. It involves not only the act of intercourse, but any sexual touches, kissing, etc. which lead up to the act. Couples who love each other should demonstrate their love by giving themselves to one another through marriage before they give their bodies through sex. True love means "only you and always you", and such a commitment is shown only through marriage. This sin injures body, soul, heart, and mind:

• First, a mortal sin is committed which causes the loss of friendship with God and the loss of eternal life.

• Second, the risk of unwanted pregnancy and the temptation to murder through abortion.

• Third, the risk of venereal disease, and AIDS.

• Fourth, the emotional pain of separation after intimate union without the commitment of marriage occurs.

7. *YOU SHALL NOT STEAL.* [2401-2463] If one steals one must make restitution and return the property if possible, or give to the poor. However, one can take food to survive when in danger of starvation.

8. *YOU SHALL NOT BEAR FALSE WITNESS AGAINST YOUR NEIGHBOR.* [2464-2513] Lying, calumny (telling the faults of someone that are untrue), and detraction (unnecessarily revealing someone's true faults) are wrong.

9. *YOU SHALL NOT COVET YOUR NEIGHBOR'S WIFE.* [2514-2533] This teaches that willful and deliberate impure thoughts are sinful. (Mt.5:27, 28)

10. *YOU SHALL NOT COVET YOUR NEIGHBOR'S GOODS.* [2534-2557] The virtue of detachment is needed to obey this commandment. Scripture warns against attachment to wealth (Mt.19:16-30, Lk.6:20-26, 12:13-31, Jas.5:1-6).

The Six Commandments of the Church
[2041-2043, 2048]

1. To attend Mass on all Sundays and Holy Days of Obligation.

2. To fast and abstain on the days appointed.

3. To confess our sins at least once a year.

4. To receive Holy Communion during the Easter Season.

5. To contribute to the support of the Church. (Give alms

according to your income to your local church, charities, and missionaries.)

6. To observe the laws of the Church regarding marriage. (Be married only with the Church's permission.)

Holy Days of Obligation
[2043, 2180, 2698]

All Sundays as well as: December 8—Immaculate Conception, Dec.25—Christmas, Jan.1—Solemnity of Mary, Ascension Thursday—40 days after Easter, August 15— Assumption of Mary, and Nov.1—All Saints Day. (In those States which have chosen the option, Ascension is Transferred from Thursday to the Seventh Sunday of Easter.)

Sins Against the Holy Spirit
[1864]

1. Presumption. 2. Despair. 3. Resisting the known truth. 4. Envy of another's spiritual good. 5. Obstinacy in sin. 6. Final impenitence.

Virtues and Vices

Virtue: [1804] A good habit; a habit of doing good and avoiding evil.

Vice: [1865]A bad habit; a habit of sin.

Seven Virtues: [1833-1844] Humility, detachment, chastity, brotherly love, temperance, meekness, diligence.

Seven Vices:　[1866, 1876]　Pride, avarice, lust, envy, gluttony, anger, sloth.

The Three Theological Virtues:
[1812-1829] Faith, Hope, and Love. (1Cor.13:13)

The Cardinal Virtues: [1805] Prudence, Temperance, Fortitude, and Justice.

The Cross
[617]

The cross is the condition of Christ's discipleship. It includes all the suffering and hardship involved in resisting temptation, keeping the commandments, and doing the physical and spiritual works of mercy. *If anyone wishes to come after me, let him deny himself, and take up his cross daily, and follow me.* (Lk.9:23,1Cor.1:18)

Concupiscence
[1264, 1426, 2515]

Concupiscence is the inclination toward sin that our nature possesses as a result of original sin. We must struggle to do good with the help of God's grace (Gen.6:5, 8:21, Mt.26:41, Rom.7:23, 8:6, Gal.5:17).

Temptation
[2846-2849]

Temptation is the lure of sin which comes from the world, the flesh, and the devil (1John2:15-17). Temptation is not a sin. In fact, if we are tempted, it is a sign that we have not yet sinned. When we are tempted, we should remember to pray, and think about the four last things: death, judgment, heaven, and hell (Mt.26:41). We are not tempted beyond our strength, provided we pray to God for help (1Cor.10:13, Gen.4:6, 7).

Faith and Works
[160-165, 1987-2029, 2443-2449]

Faith is belief in God, and faith is necessary for salvation (Heb.11:6). *Faith is the assurance of things hoped for, the evidence of things not seen.* (Heb.11:1) (1Jn.5:4, 5). God requires works of mercy to accompany faith: Jas.2:14-26, Mt.5:17-22, 7:21-23, 16:27, 19:16-19, 25:31-46, Dan.4:24, Rev.3:2, 14:13, 20:13, 1Jn.2:4, Eph.5:5-7, Gal.5:16-21, Rm.8:17. *Not every one who says to me, 'Lord, Lord,' shall enter the kingdom of heaven, but he who does the will of my Father who is in heaven.* (Mt.7:21) *If you would enter life, keep the commandments.* (Mt.19:17-19) *So faith by itself, if it has no works, is dead... You see that a man is justified by works and not by faith alone. For as the body apart from the spirit is dead, so faith apart from works is dead.* (Jas.2:14-26) We have a *firm hope and confidence* of salvation through our faith in Christ (Rom.10:9, 10, Jn.3:16, 5:24, 11:26, 17:3); however, *we cannot be absolutely certain we are saved*—we must hope for the grace of final perseverance: (Mt.10:22, 24:13, 1Cor.4:3-5, 9:26-27, 10:12, Phil.2:12, 3:10-16, Jn.15:6, Heb.6:11-12, 10:26, 2Tim.2:12, 13, Ezek.33:12-20, Rom.5:2, 8:24-25). A person can receive the gift of salvation through sanctifying grace, and then lose it through mortal sin.(1Jn.5:16, 17, Jn.15:6)

The Fourteen Good Works of Love and Mercy
[2443, 2447]

The Seven Physical Works of Mercy

1. Feed the hungry.
2. Give drink to the thirsty.
3. Clothe the naked.
4. Shelter the homeless.
5. Visit the sick.
6. Visit the imprisoned. (Mt.25:34-40)
7. Bury the dead. (Tb.1:16, 17, Acts 8:2)

The Seven Spiritual Works of Mercy

1. Counsel the doubtful (1Thess.5:9-11).
2. Instruct the ignorant (Acts8:35-39).
3. Convert or admonish the sinner
     (Acts2:40, 41, Jas.5:19, 20).
4. Comfort the sorrowful (Rom.12:15).
5. Forgive all injuries (Mt.18:21,22).
6. Bear wrongs patiently (1Cor.13:5).
7. Pray for the living and the dead (Jas.5:16, 2Mac.12:46).

The Resurrection
The angel said to the women, "Do not be afraid; for I know that
you seek Jesus who was crucified. He is not here; for he has
risen, as he said." (Matthew 28:5, 6)

The Ascension

"But you shall receive power when the Holy Spirit has come upon you; and you shall be my witnesses in Jerusalem and in all Judea and Samaria and to the end of the earth." And when he had said this, as they were looking on, he was lifted up, and a cloud took him out of their sight. (Acts 1:8, 9)

Part IV

Prayer

[2558-2561]

And I tell you, Ask, and it will be given you; seek, and you will find; knock, and it will be opened to you. (Luke 11:9)

What is Prayer?

Prayer is lifting our hearts and minds to God. Prayer is conversation with God. "Prayer is the key of Heaven," St. Augustine. Prayer is a living relationship between the children of God and their Father. Prayer is the habit of being in the presence of and in communion with the Holy Trinity. Prayer is the way the Holy Spirit, who dwells within us, inspires and helps us in our weakness to pray and love God (Rom.8:26).

Why do we pray?
[2744]

We pray so that we can go to heaven. St. Augustine says: "As our body cannot live without nourishment, so our soul cannot spiritually be kept alive without prayer." St. Alphonsus says: "He who prays, is saved; he who prays not, is damned!" Prayer is powerful: *Those who trust in you cannot be put to shame.* (Dan.3:40) *The unceasing prayer of a just man is of great avail.* (Jam.5:16-18, 2 Kings 20:1-6, Joshua 10:12-14, Daniel 6)

Where do we pray?
[2691]

We may pray at home in our room (Mt.6:1-6, Mk.1:35), at Church with our family (Mt.21:13), while riding in a car or anywhere. Through prayer, we can sanctify idle moments and give that extra free time to God.

The Four Main Purposes of Prayer
[2626-2649]

1. Adoration: Proper worship of God due to Him as our Creator.
2. Thanksgiving: Gratefulness to God for His gifts to us.
3. Reparation: To obtain pardon for sins and do penance.
4. Petition: We ask for spiritual and physical goods.

The Seven Main Qualities of Prayer
[2725-2758]

1. Devotion: (Matt.15:8)

2. Fervor: (Lk.22:43, 44)

3. Perseverance: (Lk.11:5-10, Lk.18:1-8, Matt.24:13)

4. Humility: (Jam.4:6, Matt.6:1-6, Lk.18:9-14)

5. Attention: How can we expect God to listen to our prayer, if we are not paying attention to it? (Matt.6:7, 8) Involuntary distractions in prayer are inevitable, but we should try to minimize them.

6. Faith: *Those who trust in you cannot be put to shame.* (Dan.3:40; Mat.19:26, Heb.11:6)

7. Right Priority: When we pray we need to have the right priority, namely that of God's will over our own. (Lk.22:42, Mt.6:31-33, 16:26). Does God always answer our prayers? **Yes**. There are three answers to prayer—yes, no, and please wait. No prayer is unanswered, and no prayer is unheard.

We should pray at least 5 to 15 minutes everyday. Since God is the most important "person" in our life, we should speak to Him everyday. We spend far more time each day pursuing recreation, than we do in strengthening our relationship with God. Our soul is more important than our body. And, God is certainly more important than anyone or anything else in our life. He deserves a priority of time, *pray always* (Lk.18:1, 1 Thess. 5:17, Eph. 6:18).

Basic Catholic Prayers

The Sign of the Cross

In the name of the Father, and of the Son, and of the Holy Spirit Amen.(Jn.14:14, Mt.28:19)

The Lord's Prayer
[2759-2865]

Our Father who art in heaven, hallowed be Thy name. Thy kingdom come, Thy will be done on earth, as it is in heaven. Give us this day our daily bread. And forgive us our trespasses as we forgive those who trespass against us. And lead us not into temptation, but deliver us from evil. Amen (Matthew 6:9-13)

The Hail Mary
[2673-2682]

Hail Mary, full of grace! The Lord is with thee. Blessed art thou among women, and blessed is the fruit of thy womb, Jesus. Holy Mary Mother of God, pray for us sinners, now and at the hour of our death. Amen. (Based on Luke 1:28,42 and Tradition)

The Glory Be

Glory be to the Father, and to the Son, and to the Holy Spirit.
As it was in the beginning, is now, and ever shall be, world without end. Amen.(Based on Matthew 28:19 and Tradition)

Act of Contrition

O my God, I am heartily sorry for having offended you, and I detest all my sins, because I dread the loss of heaven and the pains of hell, but most of all because they offend you, my God, who are all good and deserving of all my love. I firmly resolve, with the help of your grace, to confess my sins, to do penance, and to amend my life. Amen.

The Apostle's Creed

I believe in God the Father Almighty, Creator of heaven and earth; and in Jesus Christ, His only Son, Our Lord; Who was conceived by the Holy Spirit, born of the Virgin Mary, suffered under Pontius Pilate, was crucified, died, and was buried. He descended into hell; on the third day He arose again from the dead. He ascended into heaven, and is seated at the right hand of the Father. He will come again to judge the living and the dead. I believe in the Holy Spirit, the Holy Catholic Church, the communion of saints, the forgiveness of sins, the resurrection of the body, and life everlasting. Amen.

Hail Holy Queen

Hail Holy Queen, Mother of Mercy, our life our sweetness and our hope. To Thee do we cry, poor banished children of Eve. To Thee do we send up our sighs, mourning and weeping in this valley of tears. Turn then, most gracious advocate, thine eyes of mercy towards us, and after this our exile, show unto us the blessed fruit of Thy womb, Jesus. O clement, O loving, O sweet virgin Mary.

The Memorare

Remember, O most gracious Virgin Mary, that never was it known that anyone who fled to thy protection, implored thy help, or sought thy intercession was left unaided. Inspired with this confidence, I fly unto thee, O Virgin of virgins, my Mother. To thee I come, before thee I stand, sinful and sorrowful. O Mother of the Word Incarnate, despise not my petitions, but in thy mercy hear and answer me. Amen.

Grace Before Meals

Bless us O Lord, and these Thy gifts which we are about to receive from Thy bounty, through Christ our Lord. Amen.

Grace After Meals

We give Thee thanks, Almighty God, for these and all Thy gifts which we have received from Thy bounty through Christ our Lord. Amen.

Prayer to St. Michael the Archangel

St. Michael the Archangel, defend us in battle; be our defense against the wickedness and snares of the devil. May God rebuke him, we humbly pray; and do thou, O prince of the heavenly host, by the power of God, cast into hell Satan and all the other evil spirits who prowl about the world seeking the ruin of souls. Amen.

Prayer to My Guardian Angel

Angel of God, my guardian dear
To whom His love commits me here,
Ever this day be at my side,
To light and guard, to rule and guide. Amen.

Sacramentals
[1667-1668, 1670, 1677]

The Church has instituted Sacramentals. They are sacred signs which bear a resemblance to the sacraments. They signify effects, especially of a spiritual nature, which occur through the intercession of the Church. They help dispose us to receive the sacraments, and help render various occasions in life holy. The Rosary and the Miraculous Medal are two of the most popular Sacramentals.

Why Pray The Rosary?
[971, 2678, 2708]

The main devotion to Mary is the Rosary, a Christ-centered, biblical prayer which combines meditation on the life of Jesus and Mary with the Lord's prayer and the Hail Mary. Pope John Paul II calls the Rosary his favorite prayer. (The Rosary, Papal Teachings, Daughters of St. Paul, p. 281, 282.)

In his last year of the seminary, Father Patrick Peyton was dying of tuberculous, and he prayed the rosary asking for a cure. He recovered fully and went on to start "The Family Rosary Crusade" whose motto was: "The family that prays together stays together". Jesus taught us that we need to have

45

attention to the words we speak to God in prayer, and not simply say many words (Mt.6:7). However, the Bible teaches repetitious prayer is good see: (Mt.26:44, Psalms 117, 136, 150, Is.6:3, Rev.4:8 and Daniel 3:52-90.)

We pray to Mary because she is the Mother of God and her prayers are the most powerful. When we pray the Hail Mary we combine worship of God and honor of Mary. We unite our prayers to God with hers.

When we need help most, we don't just go directly to God alone, we ask others to pray for us and with us. When we pray the Rosary, we have Mary, the Holy Mother of God, pray to God for us and with us. God wishes us to honor Mary because of her special role in God's plan of salvation to contribute to the redemption of man, just as much as Eve contributed to the fall of man. Mary is our spiritual Mother, and we grow in grace when we honor her in a spiritual way. *Whoever glorifies his mother is like one who lays up treasure* (Sir.3:4, 5). Just as a Father is filled with joy at the love and respect others give to his children, so too, is God the Father overjoyed and seeks for us to honor His Daughter Mary, the mother of His Son Jesus, and the Mother of His Mystical Body, the Church.

We meditate on the Mysteries of the Rosary by using our imagination to picture each event occurring in front of us as we say the Hail Mary prayers. We should begin to pray the Rosary on a daily basis by praying just a decade each day, until we feel we want to pray more.

How to Pray the Rosary

1. Make the Sign of the Cross.

2. Pray the Apostle's Creed on the crucifix.

3. Pray the Lord's prayer on the first bead.

4. Pray the Hail Mary prayer on the next three beads. (The three beads are a symbol for the Trinity.)

5. Pray the Glory Be, and announce the first mystery. (Mysteries are listed below.)

6. Pray the Lord's prayer on the next bead.

7. Pray ten Hail Marys on the next ten beads while meditating on the mystery.

8. Repeat steps 5-7 again on each remaining decade. (Decade meaning the ten Hail Marys, Glory be and the Our Father, with the mystery.)

9. End by praying the Hail Holy Queen.

People usually say 5 Decades of the Rosary a day. If you find the Rosary too hard at first or don't seem to have the time, then you should start off with 1 decade a day. You may later want to pray 5 decades a day as you get used to the prayer. All who pray the Rosary should experience a profound outpouring of grace. I have a saying, "A decade a day keeps the devil away!"

The Mysteries of the Rosary

To meditate on the Mysteries we can use pictures, or use our imagination to picture the scene in our minds.

The Joyful Mysteries:
(Usually said on Monday and Thursday.)

1. The Annunciation (Lk.1:28—For humility)

2. The Visitation (Lk.1:41-42—For Love of Neighbor)

3. The Nativity (Lk.2:7—For Poverty)

4. The Presentation (Lk.2:22-23—For Obedience)

5. The Finding in the Temple (Lk.2:46—For Joy in Finding Jesus)

The Luminous Mysteries:
(Usually said on Thursdays)

6. The Baptism of Jesus (Matt.3:16-17—For Openness to the Holy Spirit)

7. The Wedding at Cana (Jn. 2:5-7—To Jesus Through Mary)

8. Proclaiming the Kingdom (Matt. 10:7-8—Repentance and Trust in God)

9. The Transfiguration (Luke 9:29-35—Desire for Holiness)

10. The Institution of the Eucharist (Luke 22:19-20—Adoration)

The Sorrowful Mysteries:
(Usually said on Tuesday and Friday)

11. The Agony in the Garden (Lk.22:44-45—For sorrow for sin)

12. The Scourging at the Pillar (Jn.19:1—For purity)

13. The Crowning with Thorns (Mt.27:28-29—For courage)

14. The Carrying of the Cross (Jn.19:17—For Patience)

15. The Crucifixion (Lk.23:46—For Perseverance)

The Glorious Mysteries:
(Usually said on Wednesday, Saturday, and Sunday)

16. The Resurrection (Mk.16:6—For Faith)

17. The Ascension (Mk.16:19—For Hope)

18. The Descent of the Holy Spirit (Acts2:4—For Love of God)

19. The Assumption of Mary (Rev.21:1—For a happy death)

20. The Coronation of Mary (Rev.21:1—For trust in Mary's Intercession)

The Fifteen Promises of the Rosary

These are the Fifteen Promises of Mary to Christians who pray the Rosary. They were given in a private revelation to St.Dominic and Blessed Alan.

1. Whoever will faithfully serve me by the recitation of the

Rosary will receive signal graces.

2. I promise my special protection and greatest graces to all those who will recite the Rosary.

3. The Rosary shall be a powerful armor against hell: it shall destroy vice, decrease sin, and defeat heresies.

4. I will cause virtue and good works to flourish; it shall obtain for souls the abundant mercy of God; it shall withdraw the hearts of men from the love of the world and its vanities and shall lift them to the desire of eternal things. Oh, that souls would sanctify themselves by this means!

5. The soul that recommends itself to me by the meditation of the Rosary shall not perish.

6. Whoever will recite the Rosary devoutly, applying himself to the consideration of its sacred mysteries, shall never be conquered by misfortune. God will not chastise him in His justice; he shall not perish by an unprovided death; if he shall be just, he shall remain in the grace of God and become worthy of eternal life.

7. Whoever will have a true devotion for the Rosary shall not die without the sacraments of the Church.

8. Those who faithfully recite the Rosary shall have during their life and at their death the light of God and the plenitude of His graces; at the moment of death they shall participate in the merits of the saints in paradise.

9. I will deliver from purgatory those who have been devoted to the Rosary.

10. The faithful children of the Rosary shall merit a high

degree of glory in heaven.

11. You shall obtain all that you ask of me by the recitation of the Rosary.

12. All those who propagate the holy Rosary shall be aided by me in their necessities.

13. I have obtained from my divine Son that all the advocates of the Rosary shall have for intercessors the entire celestial court during their lives and at the hour of their death.

14. All who recite the Rosary are my sons and brothers of my only Son, Jesus Christ.

15. Devotion to the Rosary is a great sign of predestination. (Imprimatur for 15 Promises was given by Patrick J.Hayes, D.D., Archbishop of New York)

The Miraculous Medal

The Blessed Virgin Mary spoke to St.Catherine Laboure on November 27, 1830, saying: *Have a medal struck after this image. All who wear it will receive great graces; they should wear it around the neck. Graces will abound for those who wear it with confidence.* In 1832 the first medals were being distributed in France with the church's approval. As a result of the many miracles, both spiritual and physical—conversions, healings, and protection from injuries—it quickly became known as "The Miraculous Medal". These miracles have continued since the Medal was first propagated in 1832. People who have worn the medal have become more receptive to God's grace. The medal is not magical; God has chosen to use this medal as an instrument to bring His grace to us. It is similar to the Rod of Moses (Ex.14:15-31), the

Serpent of Brass (Num.21:8, 9) and the handkerchief of
St.Paul (Acts 19:11-12). The Woman on the front of the
Medal is Mary, and she is like the Woman in Rev.12:1: *A
great sign appeared in the heavens, a woman clothed with the
sun.* A serpent who seduced Eve, is under her feet symbolizing the prophesy in Gen.3:15. Unlike Eve, Mary defeats the
serpent because she never committed sin. The Medal reads *O
Mary, conceived without sin, pray for us who have recourse
to thee.* We should try to pray this prayer each day. The
twelve stars symbolize the crown of Mary in Rev.12:1 *On her
head a crown of 12 stars,* also the 12 tribes of Israel, the 12
Apostles, and the Twelve fruits of the Holy Spirit (Gal.5:22).
The hearts on the medal symbolize the Sacred Heart of Jesus
(Matt.11:29, Jn.13:23) and the Immaculate Heart of Mary
(Lk.2:19, 35, 51), which has a sword through it symbolizing
her sorrow over the death of her Son and the sins of the
world. The Cross with the Letter M for Mary, symbolizes
how Mary and Jesus work together for our redemption as
Adam and Eve acted together for our fall from grace. The
rays from her hands symbolize the graces that fall from
heaven to earth, especially those which people ask for.

Pentecost

And there appeared to them tongues as of fire, distributed and resting on each one of them. And they were all filled with the Holy Spirit and began to speak in other tongues, as the Spirit gave them utterance. Acts 1:3, 4

A Scriptural Catechism

Appendix

Please note The Imprimatur was given only for the main text of this book, not for the Appendix. This supplemental material has its own ecclesiastical approbation independent of that of the main text.

Indulgences

Excerpt from "Catechism of the Catholic Church":
1471 The doctrine and practice of indulgences in the Church are closely linked to the effects of the sacrament of Penance.

What is an indulgence?

"An indulgence is a remission before God of the temporal punishment due to sins whose guilt has already been forgiven, which the faithful Christian who is duly disposed gains under certain prescribed conditions through the action of the Church which, as the minister of redemption, dispenses and applies with authority the treasury of the satisfaction of Christ and the saints."

"An indulgence is partial or plenary according as it removes either part or all of the temporal punishment due to sin." The faithful can gain indulgences for themselves or apply them to the dead.

-Taken from "Catechism of the Catholic Church" English Edition.

The following is from "The Handbook of Indulgences, Norms and Grants, Third Edition 1986". This lists different prayers and pious actions which bring indulgences.

Adoration of the Blessed Sacrament

A *partial indulgence* is granted the Christian faithful when they visit the Blessed Sacrament for the purpose of adoration. When this is done for at least half an hour, the indulgence is a plenary one. p. 40.

Recitation of the Marian Rosary

A *plenary indulgence* is granted when the rosary is recited in a church or oratory or when it is recited in a family, a religious community, or a pious association. A *partial indulgence* is granted for its recitation in all other circumstances. p. 79.

The Handbook of Indulgences, Norms and Grants, Authorized English Edition, Copyright 1991, Catholic Book Publishing Co., N.Y.

The Stations of the Cross

Mary and the Apostles walked through the streets of Jerusalem and recalled the sufferings Our Lord endured there. The Stations in the Church represent these places on the road to Calvary. Meditating on His Passion helps us grow in our love for Christ and sorrow for our sins which crucified him. To gain a plenary indulgence from the stations one must devoutly make the Stations of the Cross, meditating on the passion and death of the Lord. No additional prayers are required. The stations of the Cross are usually prayed publicly on Fridays during Lent, but they can be prayed privately anytime during the year. The Stations are as follows:

1. Jesus is condemned to death by Pilate. (Lk.23:24)
2. Jesus takes up His cross. (Jn.19:17)
3. Jesus falls for the first time.
4. Jesus meets His sorrowful mother.
5. Jesus is assisted by Simon the Cyrene. (Lk.23:26)
6. Veronica wipes the face of Jesus with her veil.
7. Jesus falls the second time.
8. Jesus meets the sorrowful women. (Lk.23:27-31)
9. Jesus falls the third time.
10. Jesus is stripped of His garments. (Jn.19:23-24)
11. Jesus is nailed to the cross.
12. Jesus dies on the cross. (Jn.19:30)
13. Jesus is taken down from the cross.
14. Jesus is laid in the tomb. (Jn.19:42)

Rules for Fast and Abstinence during Lent

Ash Wednesday and Good Friday are days of abstinence and also days of fast. All the Fridays of Lent are days of abstinence. The law of abstinence binds all Catholics over 14 years of age. No meat is to be eaten on days of abstinence.

The law of fasting binds all Catholics from their 18th year until the beginning of their 60th year. Only one full meal and two lighter meals are allowed on days of fast. (Canon1252)

A Scriptural Guide to the Mass

I The Liturgy of the Word

1. Introductory Rites Sign of Cross (Mt.28:19) Amen (1Chr.13:36) Greeting (2Cor.13:13, Ruth 2:4)

2. Penitential Rite A. Confiteor (Jas.5:16, 1Jn.1:9) B. Kyrie (Lk.18:13, 1Tm.1:2, Tb.8:4)

3. Gloria (Lk.2:14)

4. Opening Prayer

5. 1st Reading (Mostly Old Testament)

6. Responsorial Psalm (One of the 150 Psalms of the Old Testament)

7. Second Reading (All of the New Testament except Gospels)

8. Gospel (Matthew, Mark, Luke, John)

9. Homily (Explanation of how to live the Gospel)

10. Profession of Faith (The Creed is a communal profession of Faith in Jesus Christ, His Gospel and His Catholic Church)

11. General Intercessions (Prayer of the Faithful)(Rev.8:3-4)

II The Liturgy of the Eucharist

12. Offertory (Preparation of the Gifts) (Jn.6:35, Ps.50:23, 68:36)

13. Preface (Is.6:3, Mk.12:9-10)

14. Eucharistic Prayer I, II, III, and IV, plus those for children and for reconciliation (Consecration of Bread and Wine into the Body and Blood of Christ) (Gen.14:18, Ex.12,1Cor.5:7, Mal.1:11, Mt.26:26-28, Jn.6:25-71, 1Cor.11:23-26, Lk.24:30, 31, Acts 2:42)

15. Memorial Acclamation (1Cor.15:3-5)

16. Lord's Prayer (Mt.6:9-13)

17. Sign of Peace (Jn.14:27, 20:19, Mt.5:23, 24)

18. Lamb of God (Breaking of the Bread) (Jn.1:29, Pt.1:18-21, Mt.8:8)

19. Communion (People receive the Eucharist) (Rev.19:9)

20. Closing Prayer

21. Final Blessing and Dismissal (Lk.7:50, 24:51, 2Cor.9:15)

The Four Sins Crying To Heaven For Vengeance

1. Willful murder (Gen.4:8-16)
2. Sodomy (Gen.18:20;19:12, 13, 24, 25, Rom.1:18-32)
3. Oppression of the poor (Prov.14:31)
4. Defrauding laborers of their wages. (Jas.5:4)

Nine Ways We Can Share
In The Guilt Of Another's Sin

We may share in or cause the guilt of another's sin through
the following ways:

1. By counsel.

2. By command.

3. By consent.

4. By provocation.

5. By praise or flattery.

6. By concealment.

7. By being a partner in sin.

8. By silence.

9. By defending the ill done.

Why should I confess to a Priest?

Christ Himself gave the power to forgive sins in His
name to the Apostles and their successors. "'As the Father has
sent me, even so I send you.' And when he had said this, he
breathed on them, and said to them, "Receive the Holy Spirit.
If you forgive the sins of any, they are forgiven; if you retain
the sins of any, they are retained." (Jn.20:21-23)

Today, some mistakenly think that the priest comes
between the person and Christ, instead of understanding the
priest as a bridge to Christ. Many say:"I want to go directly to
Christ not to the priest." However, to go to the priest *is to go
directly to Christ* because the priest acts (*in persona Christi*)
in the person of Christ, in God's name (Acts 5:5). The individual priest we confess to is the visible priest, Christ is the
invisible priest who is made present and acts through the

confessor.

In the year 251A.D. St. Cyprian of Carthage wrote: "...confess even this to the priests of God in a straight-forward manner and in sorrow, making an open declaration of conscience. Thus they remove the weight from their souls. God cannot be mocked or outwitted; nor can He be deceived by any clever cunning. Indeed, he but sins the more if, thinking that God is like man, he believes that he can escape the punishment of his crime by not openly admitting his crime.... I beseech you, brethren, let everyone who has sinned **confess** his sin while he is still in this world, while his confession is still admissible, while satisfaction and **remission made through the priests are pleasing before the Lord.**" (*The Faith of the Early Fathers*, Vol.1., Rev.W.A.Jurgens, p. 219)

Some people fear going to confession because of the sacrifice involved in confessing one's sins. This sacrament functions as a tribunal of mercy and a place of spiritual healing; hence, it is necessary for the confessor to have knowledge of the sinner's heart, in order to be able to judge, absolve, cure, and heal. This sacrament involves a sincere and complete confession of sins because of its very nature, as well as an exercise in humility and self-denial. This is one of the hard-earned benefits of confession. We must remember that the road to humility is paved with humiliations. It is a blow to our pride, and a humbling experience for us to go to confession. It is a spiritual growing pain. Jesus says: "He who exalts himself will be humbled, and he who humbles himself will be exalted." (Lk.14:11, 18:14) Pride keeps us from confession. We do not want to humble ourselves before another person, and admit or confess our sins. However, confessing our sins enables us to "get it off our chest", to "let it out", and so it has psychological benefits as well. The advantage of confessing our sins to a priest as opposed to a psychologist or a close friend, is that the priest can give us God's forgiveness as well as man's. When we sin our sins affect not only our relationship with God, but our neighbor. The universe is not just us and God, it is God, my neighbor and myself. Jesus is both God and man. The priest represents both God and man, the Church of Christ and the Christ of the Church. Jesus forgave sins as a man, and men grumbled against Him. What they said about Jesus then, many say about Him now in the person of His priests: "Why does this man speak thus? It is blasphemy! Who can forgive sins but God alone?" (Mk.2:7, Lk.7:49) Some did not recognize the divinity of Christ under his humble humanity, and today some do not recognize the priesthood of Christ under His humble human instrument, the Catholic Priest.

Scripture says: "They praised God for giving such author-ity to *men* " (Matt.9:8) "Christ gave us the **ministry of reconciliation**... so we are ambassadors for Christ (2Cor.5:18, 20). We must remember that the power to forgive sins com-mitted after baptism is linked specifically to the priest (Mt.9:8,18:18, Jn.20:21-23, Jas.5:14,15). The priest is to represent Christ who is both merciful and just. Remember the Proverb: "He who conceals his sins will not prosper, but he who confesses and forsakes them will obtain mercy." (Prv.28:13)

How to go to Confession:

1. Prepare for confession by an examination of conscience followed by contrition. It is essential for the person confessing (the penitent) to be contrite. Contrition is a

heartfelt sorrow and repugnance for the sin committed, along with the intention of sinning no more. As preparation, the penitent may read from passages on God's mercy such as: Ezk.33, Lk.15, Jn.8:1-11.

2. Make the Sign of the cross. The priest may read a text of holy Scripture.

3. State how long since your last confession.

4. You must confess all mortal sins you can remember according to kind and number to the best of your ability. It is a sin to deliberately conceal any mortal sins, and this would invalidate the confession. (Acts5:5) However, don't worry about sins you can't remember.

5 Receive penance and advise.

6. Pray an act of contrition.

7. Receive absolution.

8. Go and do your penance. (2Sam.12:13, 114 1Chr.212:8-13, 1Ptr.4:8, Jas.5:20)

If you forget how to go to confession simply tell the priest and he will help you.

Statues of Mary and the Saints

Statues of Mary and the Saints are not "idols" (Ex.20:4) any more than the images of the Cherubim with wings (Ex.25:20, 37:9) which God commanded to be made for the ark are "idols". In our home, we have pictures of family members whom we love which are displayed for honor, not worship or idolatry. In Church, the house of God, we have pictures and statues of the Saints, members of God's family, whom we love. These we honor; we do not worship them.

The Parallels of Eden and Calvary

The Garden of Eden	The Hill of Calvary
Adam, "Son of God" (Lk.3:38)	Christ, "New Adam" (1Cor.15:22)
Eve (2Cor.11:3) Eve: Created without sin	Mary (Lk.1:27) Mary: Conceived without sin
Death by Eve	Life through Mary
Mother of all living (Gen.3:20)	Mother of all saved (Rev.12:17)
Temptation by Lucifer, an evil angel to Eve, a virgin.	Annunciation from the Good Angel Gabriel to Mary, a virgin.
Eve disobeys God.	Mary obeys God.
Tree of Knowledge (Gen.2:9)	Tree of the Cross (Jn.19:17)
Man and woman next to the tree at the first sin (Gen.3:6)	Man and woman next to the cross at the atonement for sin (Jn.19:26)
Forbidden to eat from the tree of life (Gen.3:22)	Christ gives us the Eucharist, the Fruit from the new tree of life—the cross. (Matt.26:26-29)

Punishment for the Sin of Adam causes the ground to bring forth thorns. (Gen.3:18)	Bearing our punishment for sin, Christ is crowned with a crown of thorns. (Mt.27:29)
An angel is placed in the Garden to keep man out. (Gen.3:24)	An angel is placed in the Garden to strengthen Christ. (Lk.22:43)
The Side of Adam opened by God gives birth to his bride, Eve, during sleep. (Gen.2:21)	The Side of Christ, pierced by a lance gives birth to His bride the Church during sleep of death. (John 19:34)
Exiled from Paradise. (Gen.3:23)	Opened the gates of Paradise (Lk.23:43)
Driven from Garden (Gen.3:23)	Entered the Garden (Jn.18:1)
Clothed after sin. (Gen.3:7, 21)	Stripped at crucifixion. (Mk.15:24)
Cain slays Abel (Gen.4:8)	The Good Thief (St.Dismas) rebukes the Bad Thief. (Lk.23:39-43)
Adam and Eve gave into evil and brought death to all their descendants.	Christ and Mary overcame evil and brought life to all their spiritual descendants.

God breathed into Adam the breath of life and he became alive. (Gen.2:7)	Christ breathed on the Apostles the Holy Spirit and the power to forgive sins, and so breathed spiritual life into dead souls. (Jn.20:22, 23)

Apparitions of Mary

The Church allows, not requires, us to believe that Mary has appeared to us on earth after her Assumption to Heaven. There are several approved apparitions (appearances) of Mary such as Guadalupe, Lourdes, and Fatima. Scripture says that other saints can appear to people on earth (Mt. 17:3, Mt. 27:52, 53). If lesser saints can appear to people on earth, how much more can Mary, the Mother of God?

The Brown Scapular

A most Popular Sacramental is the Brown Scapular.

Whosoever dies wearing this Scapular, shall not suffer eternal fire. Our Lady of Mt. Carmel to St. Simon Stock July 16, 1251.

The Scapular will be for all the sign of our Consecration to the Immaculate Heart of Mary. Pope Pius XII

Any priest may bless and enroll a person in the Brown Scapular. After this, replacement scapulars do not have to be blessed since the person has been. The Sabbatine Privilege consists of Our Lady's promise to release from Purgatory, through her special intercession, on the first Saturday after their death, those who meet these three requirements:

1. Wear the Scapular.

2. Observe Chastity according to your state in life.

3. Pray daily the Little Office of Our Lady or substitute the Rosary with permission of a confessor. All confessors were given faculty to make this substitution by Pope Leo XIII in June 1901.

The Prayer of St. Francis

Lord, make me an instrument of your peace.

Where there is hatred, let me sow love.

Where there is injury, pardon.

Where there is doubt, faith.

Where there is despair, hope.

Where there is darkness, light.

And, where there is sadness, joy.

Divine Master, grant that I may not so much seek

to be consoled, as to console;

to be understood as to understand;

to be loved as to love.

For it is in giving that we receive.

It is in pardoning that we are pardoned;

and it is in dying that we are born to eternal life.

Anima Christi

Soul of Christ, sanctify me.

Body of Christ, save me.

Blood of Christ, inebriate me.

Water from the side of Christ, wash me.

Passion of Christ strengthen me.

O good Jesus, hear me.

Within Your wounds, hide me.

Never permit me to be separated from You.

From the evil one, protect me.

At the hour of my death, call me.

And bid me come to You

That with Your saints I may praise You, forever. Amen.

By St. Ignatius of Loyola—Traditionally prayed after Holy Communion.

The Angelus

V. The angel of the Lord declared unto Mary.

R. And she conceived by the Holy Spirit. (Mt.1:20)

   Hail Mary...(Lk.1:28,42)

V. Behold the handmaid of the Lord. (Lk.1:38)

R. Be it done unto me according to Thy word. (Lk.1:38)

   Hail Mary...

V. And the Word was made flesh. (Jn.1:14)

R. And dwelt among us. (Jn.1:14)

Hail Mary...

V. Pray for us, O holy Mother of God.

R. That we may be made worthy of the promises of Christ.

Let us pray: Pour forth, we beseech Thee, O Lord, Thy grace into our hearts: that we to whom the Incarnation of Christ, Thy Son, was made known by the message of an angel, may by His Passion and Cross, be brought to the glory of His Resurrection through the same Christ our Lord. Amen.

(*Note the Angelus is traditionally said by families and friends who are together at 12 and 6 PM.)

The Regina Caeli

(Said during Eastertime, instead of The Angelus)
Queen of Heaven, rejoice, Alleluia. (Rev.12:1)
For He whom thou didst deserve to bear, Alleluia.
Hath risen as He said, Alleluia. (Mt.28:6)
Pray for us to God, Alleluia.
V. Rejoice and be glad, O Virgin Mary! Alleluia.
R. Because the Lord is truly Risen, Alleluia.

Let us pray: O God, Who, by the resurrection of Thy Son, Our Lord Jesus Christ, hast vouchsafed to make glad the whole world; grant, we beseech Thee, that through the intercession of the Virgin Mary, His Mother, we may attain the joys of eternal life. Through the same Christ Our Lord. Amen.

The Fatima Prayer:

O my Jesus, forgive us our sins, save us from the fires of hell, lead all souls to heaven, especially those in most need of thy mercy. (This prayer was given in a private apparition by

Our Lady of Fatima who requested it be added to the Rosary
after each "Glory Be".)

St. Teresa's Meditation

Let nothing disturb you.

Let nothing frighten you.

All things are passing;

God never changes.

Patient endurance obtains all things;

He who has God has everything.

God alone suffices.

The Parable of Nature
(Rom.1:19,20/Wis.13:5)

*His eyes twinkle in the stars, and His face smiles in the
flower.*

*I behold His beauty in the sunset, and His golden hair in
the wheat of the field.*

*I hear the Almighty's voice in the thunder, and sense His
anger in the storm.*

*Observe the Lord's tears in the rain, and share His cheer
in the sun shower.*

*Envision His arm in the lightning, and His finger in the
eclipse.*

*One can feel His breath in the wind, and His sweat in the
ocean spray.*

Notice His shoulders in the hills, His footprints in the valleys.

We understand His depth in the ocean, and heights of divinity in the heavens.

I touch His solidity in the firmness of rocks.

I can taste divine sweetness in the fruit of the tree and vine, I smell His aroma in the flowers and the pines.

In the clouds we picture the heavenly clothing and the supreme colors in autumn leaves.

I behold the Lord's throne in the mountains and His staff in the trees.

I see the Heavenly Father's robe in the northern lights, and His belt in the rainbow.

One can recognize divine purity in the sparkling of ice, and the riches of divinity in the earth's minerals.

Consider the stillness of the Almighty in the eye of a hurricane, or His majestic speed in the tornado.

Men encounter His moods in the seasons, and His mystery in the light of the moon.

I detect the passing of the Lord's Spirit in the twilight, and the coming of His justice with the dawn.

I discern the secrets of the Lord's salvation in the seed which dies to become a new life (Jn.12:24)—for the parable of nature is the reflection of God.—Poem by Fr. Herbert Burke

A Mini-History of the Church

Remember your leaders, who spoke to you the word of God. Consider how they ended their lives, and imitate their faith. (Hebrews 13:7)

33 A.D. Our Lord dies on the cross, and rises from the dead.

33 A.D. Pentecost, the Catholic Church is born (Acts 2).

36 A.D. St. Stephen is stoned to death, becoming the first martyr.

51 A.D. First Church Council is held in Jerusalem, presided over by the First Pope, St. Peter, who settles the first doctrinal dispute (Acts 15:7-12). This shows the biblical model the Catholic Church uses, following the decisions of Peter and his successors.

64-68 First persecution of Christians by the Emperor Nero.

67 A.D. The martyrdom of Sts. Peter and Paul. (June 29th)

70 A.D. The Destruction of the Temple as predicted in Lk.18:4-44

42 A.D.to 104 A.D. Eleven Apostles are martyred.

107 A.D. Martyrdom of St. Ignatius of Antioch, Bishop of Antioch. He was eaten by lions. His writings are the first which call the church "Catholic". His feast is October 17th.

54-305 A.D. The Ten Great Roman Persecutions—Emperor
Nero, 54-68 A.D., to the Emperor Diocletian, 284-305
A.D. During these persecutions Christians were
brutally tortured and martyred, yet the Catholic
Church continued to preach the Gospel and gain more
converts.

313 A.D. Edict of Milan—The Roman persecutions are
ended.

325 A.D. The Council of Nicea—Defines The Trinity.

389-461 A.D. St. Patrick brings the Gospel to Ireland
(Mar. 17).

431 A.D. The Council of Ephesus declared Mary "Mother of
God."

452 A.D. Pope St. Leo the Great (Nov. 10) meets Attila the
Hun face to face and convinces him not to destroy
Rome.

480-547 A.D. St. Benedict, the Father of Western Monasti-
cism, founded the Benedictine Monks. Their
motto:"Pray and labor".

521-597 A.D. St. Columba converted Scotland. (June 9).

604 A.D. St. Augustine of Canterbury was sent by Pope St.
Gregory the Great to evangelize England. Patron of
England (May 27).

722 A.D. St. Boniface goes on his mission to convert Germany.

He is the Patron Saint of Germany. (June 5)

732 A.D. The Moslem attack is stopped at the Battle of Tours.

826 A.D. St. Ansgar," Apostle of the North" (Scandanavia). (Feb.3)

825-69 A.D. Sts. Cyril and Methodius convert the Slavs. (Feb.14)

1030-79 A.D. St. Stanislaus, Bishop of Cracow, is martyred (April 11)

1054 A.D. Greek Schism occurs from a dispute over the Papacy.

1170-1221 A.D. St. Dominic founds the Dominican Order. (August 8)

1082 A.D. St. Bruno founds the Carthusian Order of Hermits. (Oct. 6)

1181-1226 A.D. St. Francis of Assisi. While praying in a ruined Church he heard Our Lord speak to him from the crucifix: "Francis my house is falling into ruin, rebuild it". He sought to rebuild the old church, but later realized our Lord meant to rebuild the spirituality of the people. His holiness attracted many disciples who were the beginnings of the Order of St. Francis. (Oct. 4)

1225-1274 A.D. St. Thomas Aquinas, Doctor of the Church, combined the philosophy of Aristotle with Catholic theology. His writings exhibit the profound unity of faith and reason. (Jan. 28)

1492 A.D. Christopher Columbus discovers America.

1517 A.D. Father Martin Luther, an Augustinian priest, proposes an misinterpretation of Romans that a man is saved by "faith alone", without charitable works or the 10 commandments. The Church disagrees (Mt.7:21-23, 19:17-19, Gal.5:16-21, Jas.2:14-26). This conflict results in a split in the church with many offshoots. The Second Vatican Council (1962) later acknowledged that blame for the split of Christianity was on both sides, Catholic and Protestant, and called for Ecumenism.

1531 A.D. Our Lady of Guadalupe appeared to an Indian convert, St. Juan Diego. Mary leaves a Miraculous Image of Herself, on display in Mexico, that still baffles scientists of our day. (Dec. 12)

1535 A.D. St. Thomas More and St. John Fisher were martyred by King Henry VIII because they refused to recognize the king, instead of the Pope, as head of the Church in England. (June 22)

1545-1563 A.D. The Council of Trent contradicts Protestant-ism. It teaches how man is justified by grace, but not faith without obedience. Charitable works and obedience to God's commandments begin and end in grace, and are a necessity for salvation.

1491-1556 A.D. St. Ignatius Loyola founds the Jesuits. (July 31)

1506-1552 A.D. St. Francis Xavier brought the gospel to Japan, the Philippines, and New Guinea. "As long as there are souls in the world who do not love God I cannot rest." (December 3)

1566-1597 A.D. St. Paul Miki and 25 companions were martyred by crucifixion in Nagasaki during the persecution by the Emperor. (Feb. 6)

1624 A.D. Alexander de Thodes, S.J., the "Apostle of Vietnam", converted many. Persecutions of Catholics later came, and there were 117 beatified as the "Martyrs of Tonkin."

1607-1646 A.D. St. Isaac Jogues, a Jesuit missionary was martyred by Mohawks near Albany, New York. (October 19)

1656-1680 A.D. Bl. Kateri Tekakwitha, "the Lily of the Mohawks", was an Indian convert who excelled in virtue. (July 14)

1647-1690 A.D. St. Margaret Mary Alacoque received the visions of the Sacred Heart of Our Lord. (Oct. 16)

1769 A.D. Bl. Junipero Serra starts a mission at San Diego (July 1).

1774-1821 St. Elizabeth Ann Seton, first American Saint (Jan. 4).

1786-1859 A.D. Holy St. John Vianney told people their sins in confession before they told him. Patron of Parish Priests (Aug 4)

1806-76 A.D. St. Catherine Laboure receives the Miraculous Medal.

1839-1846 A.D. The 79 Martyrs of Korea. (Sept. 20)

1844-79 A.D. Our Lady appears to St. Bernadette in Lourdes, France, and directs her to a spring; miraculous healings have been attributed to it ever since. Our Lady told her, "I do not promise to make you happy in this world, but in the next." St. Bernadette's feast is April 16. Our Lady of Lourdes is Feb. 11.

1854 A.D. Dec. 8 Pope Pius IX—Dogma of Immaculate Conception.

1869-71 A.D. Vatican I teaches Papal Infallibility.

1889-1956 A.D. 119 are martyred in China. Persecution of Catholics in China continues to this day under the Communists (July 9)

1890-1902 A.D St. Maria Goretti, virgin and martyr, was only 12 years old when she gave her life for Christ. A man tried to seduce her but she refused him and was stabbed to death. (July 6)

1917 A.D. The Russian Communist Revolution occurs. Communism comes to Russia, and Catholics are persecuted for their faith.

1917 A.D. Our Lady of Fatima appears to three children in Portugal six times between May 13 and Oct. 13. Our Lady requested that people pray the rosary daily and do penance for the conversion of sinners and the conversion of Russia.

1894-1941 A.D. St. Maximilian Kolbe, a Polish-born Priest who was a prisoner in Auschwitz, offered his life to the Nazis in exchange for the life of a married man with a family. (Aug. 14)

1949 A.D. The Chinese Communist Revolution occurs and outlaws the Roman Catholic Religion.

1951 A.D. Archbishop Fulton J. Sheen becomes the first Christian Minister to have a TV show, it's called, "Life is Worth Living."

1962-65 A.D. The Council of Vatican II calls for Reforms in the liturgy. The Church later allows translations of the revised Latin mass to the vernacular or native tongue. It calls for a new dialogue of ecumenism with the Orthodox and the Protestants, who are now to be called "separated brethren." It also reaffirms the Church's teaching on celibacy for the priesthood, and the sins of contraception (GS51) and abortion (GS51).

1963 A.D. U.S. Supreme Court forces prayer out of public schools.

1968 A.D. Pope Paul VI reaffirms Church's teaching against contraception in his Encyclical "Humanae Vitae."

1969 A.D. The evil of Hardcore Pornography begins in America.

1973 A.D. *Roe v. Wade* decision: The Supreme Court in the U.S. allows abortion to be performed through the full 9 months of pregnancy. Each year in our nation's capital on January 22 the March for Life is held to protest the death of the unborn.

1992 A.D. The "Catechism of the Catholic Church" is issued by Pope John Paul II. All catechisms are to be in conformity with it.

The Twelve Promises of the Sacred Heart

Given by Our Lord in a private revelation to St. Margaret Mary Alacoque in 1675:

1. I will give them all the graces necessary in their state in life.

2. I will establish peace in their homes.

3. I will comfort them in all their afflictions.

4. I will be their secure refuge during life and, above all, in death.

5. I will bestow abundant blessings upon all their undertakings.

6. Sinners shall find in My Heart the source and the infinite ocean of mercy.

7. By devotion to My Heart tepid souls shall grow fervent.

8. Fervent souls shall quickly mount to high perfection.

9. I will bless every place where a picture of My Heart shall be set up and honored.

10. I will give to priests the gift of touching the most hardened hearts.

11. Those who promote this devotion shall have their names written in My Heart, never to be blotted out.

12. I will grant the grace of final penitence to those who receive Holy Communion on the first Friday of nine consecutive months.

The Litany of the Sacred Heart

Come to me, all who labor and are heavy laden, and I will give you rest. Take my yoke upon you, and learn from me; for I am gentle and lowly in heart, and you will find rest for your souls. For my yoke is easy, and my burden light. Mt. 11:28-30

Voice:	*Response:*
Lord, have mercy,	*Lord, have mercy*
Christ, have mercy	*Christ, have mercy*
Lord, have mercy	*Lord, have mercy*
God our Father in heaven	*have mercy on us*
God the Son, Redeemer of the world	*have mercy on us*
God the Holy Spirit	*have mercy on us*

Holy Trinity, one God   *have mercy on us*

Heart of Jesus, Son of the eternal Father   *have mercy on us*

Heart of Jesus, formed by the Holy Spirit   *have mercy on us*

   in the womb of the Virgin Mother   *have mercy on us*

Heart of Jesus, one with the eternal Word   *have mercy on us*

Heart of Jesus, infinite in majesty   *have mercy on us*

Heart of Jesus, holy temple of God   *have mercy on us*

Heart of Jesus, tabernacle of the Most High

                                 have mercy on us

Heart of Jesus, house of God and gate of heaven

                                 have mercy on us

Heart of Jesus, aflame with love for us   *have mercy on us*

Heart of Jesus, source of justice and love   *have mercy on us*

Heart of Jesus, full of goodness and love   *have mercy on us*

Heart of Jesus, well-spring of all virtue   *have mercy on us*

Heart of Jesus, worthy of all praise   *have mercy on us*

Heart of Jesus, king and center of all hearts

                                 have mercy on us

Heart of Jesus, treasure-house of wisdom and knowledge

                                 have mercy on us

Heart of Jesus, in whom there dwells the fullness of divinity

                                 have mercy on us

Heart of Jesus, in whom the Father well pleased

                                 have mercy on us

Heart of Jesus, from whose fullness we have all received
                                        have mercy on us

Heart of Jesus, desire of the eternal hills   have mercy on us

Heart of Jesus, patient and full of mercy   have mercy on us

Heart of Jesus, generous to all who turn to you
                                        have mercy on us

Heart of Jesus, fountain of life and holiness
                                        have mercy on us

Heart of Jesus, atonement for our sins   have mercy on us

Heart of Jesus, overwhelmed with insults   have mercy on us

Heart of Jesus, broken for our sins   have mercy on us

Heart of Jesus, obedient even to death   have mercy on us

Heart of Jesus, pierced by a lance   have mercy on us

Heart of Jesus, source of all consolation   have mercy on us

Heart of Jesus, our life and resurrection   have mercy on us

Heart of Jesus, our peace and reconciliation
                                        have mercy on us

Heart of Jesus, victim for our sins   have mercy on us

Heart of Jesus, salvation of all who trust in you
                                        have mercy on us

Heart of Jesus, hope of all who die in you have mercy on us

Heart of Jesus, delight of all the saints   have mercy on us

Lamb of God, you take away the sins of the world
                                        have mercy on us

Lamb of God, you take away the sins of the world
                                        have mercy on us

Lamb of God, you take away the sins of the world
                                        have mercy on us

V. Jesus, gentle and humble of heart.

R. Touch our hearts and make them like yours
                                        have mercy on us

Let us pray.

Father, we rejoice in the gifts of love we have
received from the heart of Jesus your Son.
Open our hearts to share his life
and continue to bless us with his love.
We ask this in the name of Jesus the Lord.

                              R. Amen.